Contents

Hair Frills

Dress up the most basic of hair pieces with these quick and easy slide-on accessories. Better yet—make frills to match some of the other pieces you're knitting. Shown here with headband for Flower Frill and hair clip for both the Bow Frill and Pomtastic Frill.

Size
one size

Gauge
22 sts and rows per 4" (10 cm) in stockinette

Yarn
• Lightweight wool, acrylic, or blend

Flower Frill
• 3 colors: A, B, and C

Bow Frill
• 2 colors: D and E

Pomtastic Frill
• 3 colors: G, H, and F

Tools
• set of size 5 (3.75 mm) DPNs

Notions
• headband or hair-clip for each Frill

• hot glue for securing items if desired

Flower Frill

Outer Layer

With A, CO 6 sts. Divide these sts evenly among 3 DPNs. PM and join to work in the round, being careful not to twist stitches.

Knit 1 round.

Increase Round: *K1, m1; rep from * around.

Repeat last 2 rows a total of 4 times—96 sts.

Knit 4 rounds.

Increase Round: *Kf&b&f in one st; rep from * around—288 sts.

Knit 3 rounds.

BO all sts.

Middle Layer

With B, CO 6 sts. Divide these sts evenly among 3 DPNs. PM and join to work in the round, being careful not to twist stitches.

Knit 1 round.

Increase Round: *K1, m1; rep from * around.

Repeat last 2 rows a total of 3 times—48 sts.

Knit 2 rounds.

Increase Round: *Kf&b&f in one st; rep from * around—144 sts.

Knit 3 rounds.

BO all sts.

Center

With C, CO 6 sts. Divide these sts evenly among 3 DPNs. PM and join to work in the round, being careful not to twist stitches.
Knit 1 round.

Increase Round: *K1, m1; rep from * around—12 sts.

Knit 1 round. Cut yarn, weave through rem sts and secure. Use a tapestry needle to weave loose ends to cast-on side of ball and tie firmly to flatten.

Tube

With C, CO 4 sts to a DPN. Work I-cord for 5 rounds. BO all sts.

Finishing

Use long tails from Center to attach all three layers of flower. Then thread these tails to inside of Tube, weaving in and out several times for sturdiness, making sure to leave tube open. Tie off tails inside tube. Weave in all loose ends. Slide tube onto hairband or hairclip. If needed, secure with more yarn and tapestry needle or hot glue.

Bitty Dots

(worked over a multiple of 4 sts)

Round 1: *With D, k1, with E, k1, with D, k2; rep from * around.

Rounds 2–3: With D, knit.

Round 4: *With D, k3, with E, k1; rep from * around.

Round 5–6: With D, knit.

Bow Frill

With D and a single DPN, CO 20 sts. With 2 DPNs, *sl 1 st to first DPN and next st to second DPN; repeat from * until all sts are divided evenly onto two DPNs. PM and join to work in the round. Knit 1 round.

Next Round: K10, pm, k to end.

Increase Round: *K1, m1R, k to one st before marker, m1L, k1; rep from * once more—24 sts.

Work even in Bitty Dots until piece measures 3 inches from CO edge.

Cut yarn for E.

Decrease Round: With D, *k2tog, k to 2 sts before marker, ssk; rep from * once more—20 sts.

Knit 3 rounds.

Flip piece inside out and weave in tails from B into the inside of the tie. Flip piece right side out.

Arrange sts so that the first 10 sts are on one DPN, and the second 10 are on another. Graft using Kitchener Stitch.

Knot

With D, CO 7 sts.

Sl first st of every row, and work back and forth in St st in until piece measures 2 inches from CO edge. BO all sts. Cut yarn, leaving long tail for sewing.

Squeeze the middle of the bowtie and tightly wrap knot strip around it. Seam knot ends together.

Slide onto hairband or hairclip. If needed, secure with more yarn and tapestry needle or hot glue.

Pomtastic Frill

Tube

With F, CO 4 sts. Work I-cord for 5 rounds. BO all sts. Weave in all loose ends.

Pom-Poms (See page 17)

With F, make a 2"(5 cm) pom-pom with 50 wraps.

With G, make a 1"(2.5 cm) pom-pom with 30 wraps.

With H, make a 1"(2.5 cm) pom-pom with 30 wraps.

Use tapestry needle to thread tails from each pom-pom into the tube and secure inside by tying a knot.

Slide onto hairband or hairclip. If needed, secure with more yarn and tapestry needle or hot glue.

Pom-poms

Feel free to use your own pom-pom making tool, or make a different size pom-pom! Here are some directions in case you need a little guidance. Cut two circles the size of the desired pom-pom from a piece of cardboard. Cut a ½-inch hole in the center of both circles. Thread a tapestry needle with a long length of yarn. Wrap yarn around the outside edge of the cardboard circle, passing it through the center hole each time. When the entire outside edge of the circle is covered with yarn, slide a scissors between the two cardboard circles and cut the yarn along the outside edge. Cut another 6-inch piece of yarn and slide it between the cardboard circles, wrapping it twice around the middle of your bundle, tie tightly and double knot (at least). Remove cardboard circles. Voila! Now just use your scissors to trim up and shape the pom-pom.

Stripey Headband

This Boho-inspired headpiece is completely adjustable and whips up quickly. It's worked back and forth and has a crocheted edging and braided tassels to secure it. Make one, two, three, or more headbands in different color and stitch-pattern combinations. She can wear it with her favorite pair of flared pants ... or, better yet, you can make a headband to match a pair of leggings from the book!

Size
one size

Band Width
2" (5 cm)

Band Length
11" (28 cm)

Gauge
20 sts and 28 rows per 4" (10 cm) in stockinette stitch

Yarn
- Medium-weight yarn in 2 colors

Tools
- size 7 (4.5 mm) needles
- size H (5 mm) crochet hook

Choppy Stripes

Row 1 (RS): With A, *k2tog twice, kf&b twice; rep from * to end.

Row 2: With A, purl.

Row 3: With B, *k2tog twice, kf&b twice; rep from * to end.

Row 4: With B, purl.

CHOPPY STRIPES

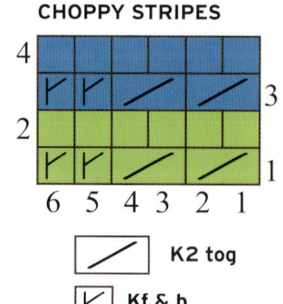

K2 tog

Kf & b

Begin

With A, CO 8 sts.

Purl 1 row. Do not cut yarn.

Switch to B.

Increase Row: K1, m1L, k to last st, m1R, k1—2 sts increased.

Purl 1 row. Do not cut yarn.

Switch to A. Work last 2 rows a total of 3 times, switching colors every 2 rows—14 sts.

Next row (RS): K1, work in Choppy Stripes pattern to last st, k1.

Work in Choppy Stripes as established until band measures 10" (25 cm) from CO edge, ending after a WS row. Discontinue Choppy Stripes, but continue switching colors every 2 rows during decreases.

Decrease Row: K1, ssk, knit to last 3 sts, k2tog, k1—2 sts decreased.

Purl 1 row.

Work last 2 rows a total of 3 times—8 sts.

BO all sts.

Finishing

With A, work single crochet around entire band as follows:

Make slip knot and place on crochet hook. *Insert hook into an edge stitch, yarn over hook, and draw a loop through stitch, yarn over hook, then draw it through both loops on hook. Rep from * for single crochet.

Braided Tassels

(make 3 at each end)

With B, cut 18 strands that measure 36" (91 cm). Use crochet hook to pull 3 strands at a time between single crocheted border and edge of headband—6 strands. Hold two strands together and braid to last 2 inches (5 cm). Tie a knot and trim ends.

Weave in all loose ends. Block.

Mini Backpack

This backpack is perfect for holding all their treasures. It's worked from the bottom up, mostly in the round, and features just a smidge of intarsia during a short-row section in either a unisex or girly option. If intarsia isn't your thing, consider striping the pack (easier yet, use a self-striping yarn!) The pack is finished with I-cord edging, a drawstring, and a toggle to keep things safely inside. Shown here with the Flower Chart.

Size
one size

Gauge
20 sts and 28 rows per 4" (10 cm) in stockinette stitch

Yarn
• Medium-weight yarn in 4 colors: A, B, C, and D

Tools
• size 7 (4.5 mm) 16" (40.6 cm) circular needles

• size 5 (3.75 mm) DPNs

• size H (5 mm) crochet hook

• sewing needle

• matching thread

Notions
• 2" (5 cm) toggle button

Base

With A and larger needles, provisionally CO 36 sts. Work back and forth in St st for 3" (7.5 cm).

Place provisionally CO sts on spare needle, ready to work RS.

Sides

Knit 18 sts on working needles, pm for end of round, k18, pick up and knit 15 sts along side, pm, knit across 36 sts from provisionally CO edge, pm, pick up and knit 15 sts along side. Join to work in the round—102 sts.

Work in the round for 1" (2.5).

Work short rows (see W&T, page 13) as follows:

Short Rows 1–2: Knit to second marker, W&T, purl to marker, W&T.

Short Rows 3–4: Knit to first marker, k8, pm, work Flower or Plane intarsia chart over 23 sts, pm, knit to next marker, knit to wrapped st, pick up wrap and work together with next st, W&T, work as established back to first marker, pick up wrap & work together with next st, W&T.

Repeat Short Rows 3–4 a total of 14 times, working intarsia chart once and removing markers when finished.

Resume working in the round once short rows are complete.

Next Round: K18, pm, k66, pm, k18.

Decrease Round: Knit to marker, sm, k2tog, k to 2 sts before marker, ssk, sm, k to end of round—2 sts decreased.

Work Decrease Round every other round a total of 12 times—78 sts.

Work even for 4 rounds.

Eyelet Round: *K4, yo, k2tog; rep from * around.

Work even for 4 rounds.

Next Rnd: Removing markers as you go, knit to second marker, sl previous 42 sts to holder—36 sts.

Front Flap

Knit 4 rows.

Decrease Row (RS): K1, ssk, k to last 3 sts, k2tog, k1—2 sts decreased.

Work Decrease Row every RS row a total of 10 times—16 sts.

Flap Edging

Place 42 sts from top of bag on spare needle, ready to work RS. Place 16 sts from front of flap on spare needle. With C and RS facing, pick up and knit 18 sts on right side of flap, k16 sts on front of flap, pick up and knit 18 sts on left side of flap, knit across 42 sts for top of bag—92 sts. Join as though to work in the round.

Using I-cord bind-off method (page 13), BO all sts.

W&T

1 Wrap and turn for short row shaping. When next st is to be knit: After working last st, with yarn in back sl next st purlwise onto RH needle.

2 Move yarn to front then sl st back onto LH needle.

3 Turn and work back as directed

I-cord Bind-Off

Hold work with RS facing, ready to BO. CO 3 sts. *K2, ssk (last I-cord st with next st of edge being bound off). Sl 3 sts now on DPN back to LH needle. Repeat from * for bind-off.

Provisional Cast-On

1 With a contrasting yarn, make a slip knot then chain 2 or 3 stitches with crochet hook. Hold a knitting needle in your left hand, over the working yarn that is coming from the crochet hook in your right hand. Take the hook over the needle, wrap the yarn over the hook, and pull it through the loop on the hook, making a chain.

2 Reposition the working yarn under the needle, and make another stitch over the needle. Continue until you have made the required number of stitches.

3 Chain two or three stitches with just the crochet hook, cut the yarn, and pull the end through. Make a knot in the beginning tail, so that you know to pull the end without the knot when it comes time to unravel the provisional cast-on.

4 Drop the contrast yarn and, starting with the first row, knit the stitches with your project yarn. When you are ready to knit from the cast-on edge, release the stitches of the contrast yarn and pick up the live stitches with your knitting needle.

Straps

Use 2 DPNs and B to work back and forth for each strap as follows:

Pick up and knit 5 sts at back top corner of bag. Work in I-cord (below) until strap measures 18" (46 cm). BO all sts. Seam bottom of strap to corresponding bottom corner.

Drawstring

Use 2 DPNs and C to work back and forth for drawstring as follows: CO 3 sts. Work in I-cord (below) until drawstring measures 20" (51 cm) from CO. BO all sts.

Buttonhole

Use 2 DPNs and C to work back and forth for "buttonhole" as follows: CO 3 sts. Work in I-cord until piece measures 3" (7.5 cm) from CO edge. BO all sts. Sew each end of I-cord, making a loop, to underside of front center panel.

Finishing

Weave in all loose ends. Block. Starting at front corner, weave drawstring in and out of eyelets. Tie a cute little bow. Using sewing needle and matching thread, sew button to front flap about halfway between top of intarsia chart and drawstring.

- -

I-cord

Cast on or pick up the required number of stitches on a double-pointed needle. Knit the stitches with another double-pointed needle, but don't turn the work.

1 Slide the stitches to the opposite end of the needle.

2 Pull the working yarn tight across the back of the stitches and knit another row.

3 Repeat this many times, forming a tiny knitted tube. To keep the stitches looking uniform, tug on the tube every few rows.

FLOWER INTARSIA CHART

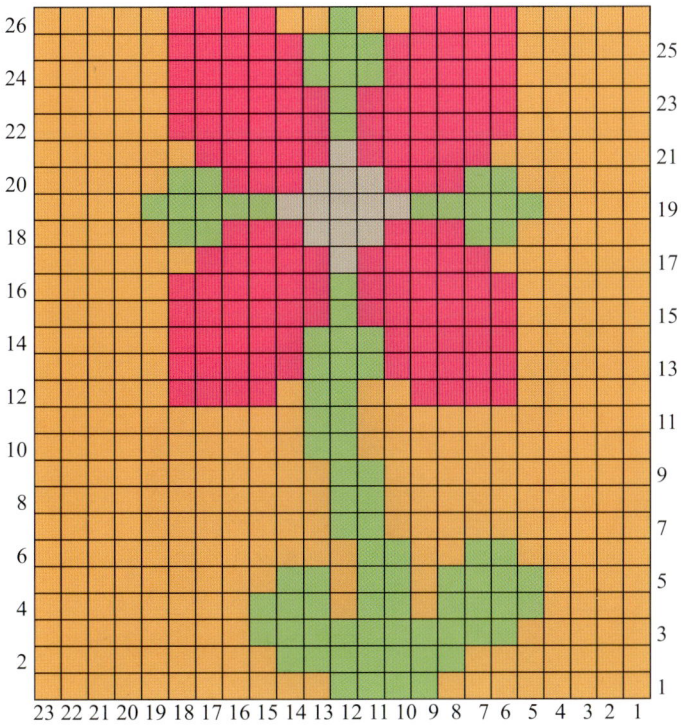

PLANE INTARSIA CHART

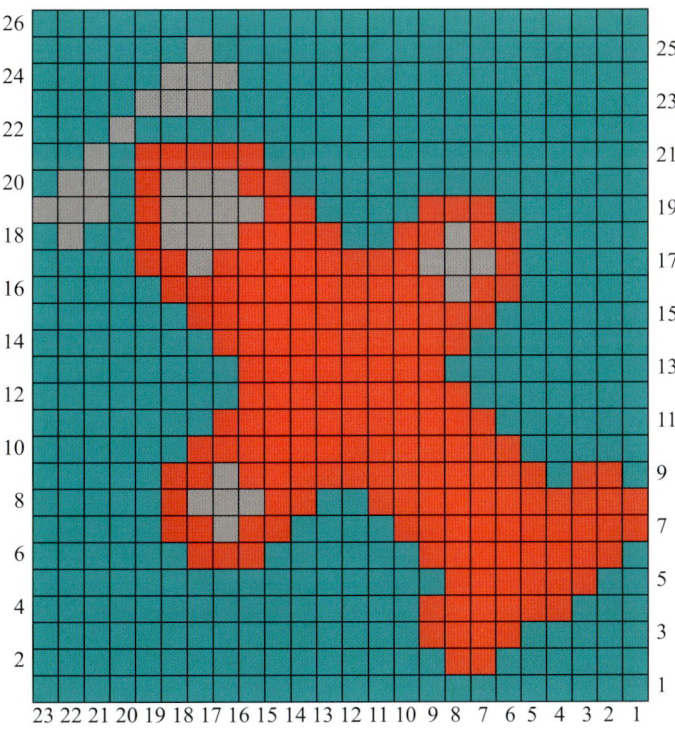

Reversible Scarf

This cozy scarf looks just as good on one side as the other because the blocks alternate between stockinette and reverse stockinette. Knit it in as many or few colors as you'd like. It will fit everyone in the house, so be sure to get extra yardage so you can make one for everyone.

Size
one size

Width
6" (15 cm)

Length
65" (165 cm)

Gauge
17 sts and 21 rows per 4" (10 cm) in stockinette stitch

Yarn
- Medium-weight wool, acrylic, or blend in 4 colors

Tools
- size 8 (5 mm) needles
- size H (5 mm) crochet hook

Pattern notes
The chart shows the color changes used in the sample. Refer to the chart for color and stitch changes.

Scarf

CO 25 sts. Purl 1 WS row.

Block 1

Work back and forth in St st until piece measures 5" (12.5 cm), ending after a WS row. Cut yarn. Switch to new color.

Block 2

Color Changing Row: *K1, p1; rep from * around.

Next row (WS): Knit.

Work back and forth in Rev St st (purl the RS rows and knit the WS rows) until second block measures 5" (12.5 cm), ending after a RS row. Cut yarn. Switch to new color.

Block 3

Work Color Changing Row from Block 2.

Next row (RS): Knit.

Work back and forth in St st until third block measures 5" (12.5 cm), ending after a WS row. Cut yarn. Switch to new color.

Work Blocks 2 and 3 a total of 6 times (13 blocks), using the chart as a guide for color and stitch pattern changes. BO all sts.

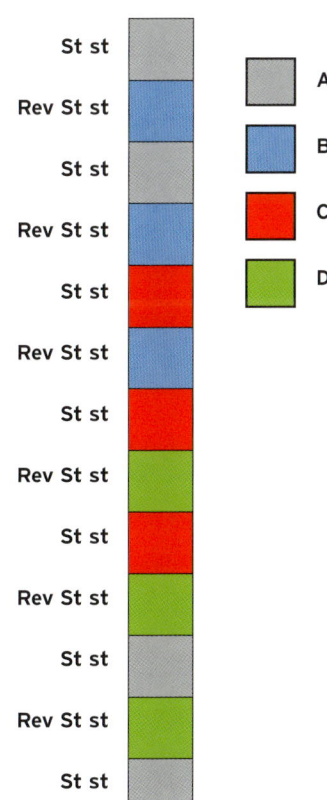

St st	▇ (grey)	
Rev St st	▇ (blue)	▇ A (grey)
St st	▇ (grey)	▇ B (blue)
Rev St st	▇ (blue)	▇ C (red)
St st	▇ (red)	▇ D (green)
Rev St st	▇ (blue)	
St st	▇ (red)	
Rev St st	▇ (green)	
St st	▇ (red)	
Rev St st	▇ (green)	
St st	▇ (grey)	
Rev St st	▇ (green)	
St st	▇ (grey)	

Finishing

Edging

With C and crochet hook, begin at one corner of the scarf and work single crochet (page 9) around entire edge of scarf. To make the scarf fully reversible and symmetrical on both sides, crochet into middle of the edge stitch instead of leaving a selvedge edge. Do not break yarn at corners.

Tassels

Cut 25 lengths of yarn, each measuring 8" (20 cm). Fold each strand in half and use crochet hook to draw the loop at the middle through one stitch on one short end of the scarf. Pull both ends of the strand through the loop snugly. Repeat for each strand, on each stitch. Trim tassels so that ends are even. Repeat process for other end of scarf.

Block.

Legwarmers

Asymmetry makes these warmers pop. They are worked top down in the round and accentuated with a skinny cabled rib. Utility doesn't end at the calves, either—try these versatile warmers on the wrists, too. Shown here in toddler size.

Size
toddler (child, tween)

Width (unstretched)
6½(7¼, 8)" [16.5(18, 20) cm]

Length
8¼(10, 12)" [21(25, 30) cm]

Gauge
20 sts and 25 rows per 4" (10 cm) in stockinette stitch

Yarn
• Medium-weight wool in 3 colors

Tools
• set of size 7 (4.5 mm) DPNs

• stitch marker

Crossover Rib

(worked over a multiple of 4 sts)

Rounds 1–2: *K2, p2; rep from * around.

Round 3 (Crossover Round): *X2, p2; rep from * around.

CROSSOVER RIB

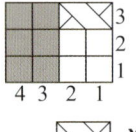

 X2

Uneven Stripes

(worked over 8 rounds)

Rounds 1–2: Work in B.

Round 3: Work in C.

Rounds 4–5: Work in B.

Rounds 6–8: Work in C.

UNEVEN STRIPES

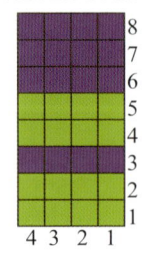

Little Zigzag

(worked over an even number of sts)

Rounds 1–2: With A, knit.

Round 3: *With A, k1, with C, k1; rep from * around.

Round 4: *With C, k1, with A, k1; rep from * around.

LITTLE ZIGZAG

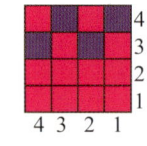

Striped Legwarmer

Calf Cuff

With A, CO 32 (36, 40) sts. Divide evenly among 3 DPNs. PM and join to work in the round.

Work the three rounds of Crossover Rib a total of 2 (3, 4) times. Work one more round in 2x2 rib. Cut yarn.

Leg

Work 1 round in Uneven Stripes pattern.

Decrease Round: Working next round in Uneven Stripe pattern as established, k1, k2tog, work to last three stitches, ssk, k1—2 sts decreased.

Continuing Uneven Stripes pattern as established, repeat Decrease Round on next round and every 10 (12, 14) rounds 3 more times—24 (28, 32) sts, ending after Round 2 or 5 of Uneven Stripes Pattern. Cut yarn.

Ankle Cuff

With A, knit 1 round. Work Rounds 2 and 3 of Crossover Rib, work Rounds 1–3 1 (2, 3) more times, then work Rounds 1 and 2 once more. BO all sts.

Zigzag Legwarmer

Calf Cuff

With B, work Calf Cuff as for Striped Legwarmer. Cut yarn.

Leg

Work 1 round in Little Zigzag pattern.

Decrease Round: Working next round in Little Zigzag pattern as established, k1, k2tog, work to last three stitches, ssk, k1—2 sts decreased.

Note: If Decrease Round is worked during either Round 3 or 4 of Little Zigzag pattern, make sure to adjust the following round so that contrasting colors are worked on alternating sts when compared to the previous round.

Continuing Little Zigzag pattern as established, repeat Decrease Round every 10 (12, 14) rounds 3 more times—24 (28, 32) sts, ending after Round 2 of Little Zigzag pattern. Cut yarn.

Ankle Cuff

With B, work Ankle Cuff as for Striped Legwarmer.

Finishing

Weave in all loose ends. Block.

Bracelet Casings

Here are some options for bracelets to play dress up! Each is a quick knit and stitch pattern options vary from colorwork to cables to texture. Casings are worked in the round and seamed around bracelet after bind off. No shaping is involved making it easy to substitute other stitch pattern options.

Cabled Casing

Size
one size

Finished Circumference
9" (23 cm)

Gauge
32 sts per 4" (10 cm) in Cable Circles

Yarn
• 35 yds (32 m) fingering weight yarn

Tools
• size 2 (2.75 mm) set of 5 DPNs

Notions
• plastic bangle bracelet

Textured Casing

Size
one size

Finished Circumference
10¾" (27 cm)

Gauge
24 sts per 4" (10 cm) in Moss Stitch, with yarn held double

Yarn
• 90 yds (82 m) fingering weight yarn

Tools
• size 4 (3.5 mm) set of 5 DPNs

Notions
• plastic bangle bracelet

Striped Casing

Size
one size

Finished Circumference
10½" (26.5 cm)

Gauge
20 sts per 4" (10 cm) in stockinette stitch

Yarn
• 15 yds (14 m) each A & B worsted weight yarn

Tools
• size 7 (4.5 mm) set of 5 DPNs

Notions
• plastic bangle bracelet

CABLED CASING

Chart columns numbered 8 7 6 5 4 3 2 1 (bottom), rows numbered 1–12 (right side)

Legend:
- T3B
- T3F
- C4F

Crossing Cable Circles

(worked over a multiple of 8 sts)

Round 1: *P2, k4, p2; rep from * around.

Round 2: *P1, T3B, T3F, p1; rep from * around.

Round 3: *P1, k2, p2, k2, p1; rep from * around.

Round 4: *T3B, p2, T3F; rep from * around.

Rounds 5–7: *K2, p4, k2; rep from * around.

Round 8: *T3F, p2, T3B; rep from * around.

Round 9: *P1, k2, p2, k2, p1; rep from * around.

Round 10: *P1, T3F, T3B, p1; rep from * around.

Round 11: *P2, k4, p2; rep from * around.

Round 12: *P2, C4F, p2; rep from * around.

Cabled Casing

CO 72 sts. Divide sts evenly among 3 DPNs. PM and join to work in the round, being careful not to twist stitches.

Work in Crossing Cable Circles until piece measures twice the width of your bangle bracelet from CO edge, ending after Round 11 of Crossing Cable Circles. Sample bracelet shown is approximately ½" (1 cm) wide, so casing was knit to 1" (2.5 cm) from CO edge. BO all sts.

Slip casing over bracelet and fold in half. Seam CO and BO edges together.

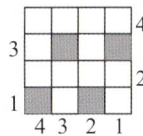

Moss Stitch

Round 1: *K1, p1; rep from * around.

Round 2: Knit.

Round 3: *P1, k1; rep from * around.

Round 4: Knit.

CO 64 sts. Divide sts evenly among 3 DPNs. PM and join to work in the round, being careful not to twist stitches.

Work in Moss Stitch until piece measures twice the width of your bangle bracelet from CO edge, ending after an odd numbered round. Sample bracelet shown is approximately 2¼" (6 cm) wide, so casing was knit to 4½" (11 cm) from CO edge. BO all sts.

Slip casing over bracelet and fold in half. Seam CO and BO edges together.

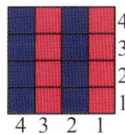

Vertical Stripes

All Rounds: *With A, k1, with B, k1; rep from * around.

With A, CO 52 sts. Divide sts evenly among 3 DPNs. PM and join to work in the round, being careful not to twist stitches.

Work in Vertical Stripes pattern until piece measures twice the width of your bangle bracelet from CO edge. Sample bracelet shown is approximately 1¼" (3 cm) wide, so casing was knit to 2½" (6 cm) from CO edge. BO all sts.

Slip casing over bracelet and fold in half. Seam CO and BO edges together.

Love Mitts

Picot hems set off these fingerless, thumbless mitts. They are worked back and forth to allow for intarsia and have just enough shaping to help hold them in place on the wrist before flaring out over the hand. If you prefer to work seamlessly, try working the mitts in the round with striping instead. Shown here in child size.

Size
toddler (child, teen)

Finished Circumference
6 (7, 8)" [15 (18, 20) cm]

Length
5½ (6, 6½)" [14 (15, 16.5) cm]

Gauge
20 sts and 26 rows per 4" (10 cm) in stockinette stitch

Yarn
• Medium-weight wool in 3 colors

Tools
• size 7 (4.5 mm) needles

Pattern Notes
Choose the size that is closest to actual hand circumference.

Wrist

With A, CO 23 (27, 31) sts.

Beginning with a WS row, work 3 rows in St st.

Eyelet Row (RS): K1, *yo, k2tog; rep from * to end of row.

Work 5 rows in St st.

Fold work so that eyelet row becomes a picot edge top of cuff.

Joining Row (RS): Join working sts to cast on edge as follows, *with left needle, pick up st from the cast on edge opposite next working st and k2tog with next working st; repeat from * to end of row.

Next Row (WS): P2 (4, 6), pm, p to last 2 (4, 6) sts, pm, p to end.

Heart Intarsia

Note: This section includes work to be done AT THE SAME TIME. Read entire section before beginning.

Increase Row (RS): K1, m1L, work to last st, m1R, K1—2 sts increased.

Work Increase Row every RS row a total of 2 (4, 5) times—31 (35, 41) sts.

AT THE SAME TIME, during first (second, third) Increase Row, begin Heart Intarsia chart over center 19 sts between markers. Work rows 1–18 of Heart Intarsia chart once.

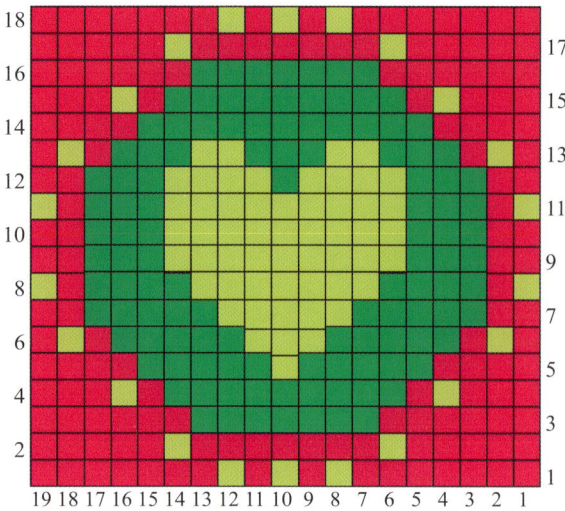

Hand

Work even until mitt measures 5½ (6, 6½)" [14 (15, 16.5) cm] from picot edge.

Work Eyelet Row once more.

Work 5 rows. BO all sts.

Finishing

Fold top edge with WS together and seam to create top picot hem. Seam sides. Weave in all loose ends. Block.

Abbreviations

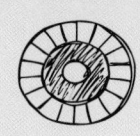

" :	inch(es)
[ ] :	rep instructions between brackets as many times as indicated
BO:	bind off
CO:	cast on
DPN(s):	double pointed needle(s)
K, k:	knit
LH:	left hand
mm:	millimeter
P, p:	purl
Pat:	pattern
PM:	place marker
Rep:	repeat
Rem:	remaining
Rev St st:	reverse stockinette stitch; purl all sts on the right side, knit all sts on the wrong side
RH:	right hand
RS:	right side
Sl:	slip
SM:	slip marker
St st:	stockinette stitch; knit all sts on the right side, purl all sts on the wrong side
St(s):	stitch(es)
WS:	wrong side
WYIF:	with yarn in front

Increases

Kf&b:	knit into the front and back of the same stitch
Kf&b&f:	knit into the front and back and front of the same stitch
M1:	make 1 st
M1L:	make 1 left-leaning st
M1R:	make 1 right-leaning st
YO:	yarn over
YFON:	yarn forward over needle

Decreases

K2tog:	knit two sts together
P2tog:	purl two sts together
Ssk:	slip 2 sts knitwise, knit these 2 sts together

Cabling

X2:	Crossover: slip 1 st to cable needle and hold to front, k1, k1 from cable needle
T3B:	slip 1 st to cable needle and hold to back, k2, p1 from cable needle
T3F:	slip 2 sts to cable needle and hold to front, p1, k2 from cable needle
C4B:	slip 2 sts to cable needle and hold to back, k2, k2 from cable needle
C4F:	slip 2 sts to cable needle and hold to front, k2, k2 from cable needle
T4B:	slip 2 sts to cable needle and hold to back, k2, p2 from cable needle
T4F:	slip 2 sts to cable needle and hold to front, p2, k2 from cable needle
C6B:	slip 3 sts to cable needle and hold to back, k3, k3 from cable needle
C6F:	slip 3 sts to cable needle and hold to front, k3, k3 from cable needle
C12B:	slip 6 sts to cable needle and hold to back, k6, k6 from cable needle
C12F:	slip 6 sts to cable needle and hold to front, k6, k6 from cable needle